# HULL

## XANDRIA PHILLIPS

Nightboat Books
New York

ISBN: 978-1-64362-008-4

Cover art: "Linear Compounds," gouache on canvas by Xandria Phillips
Cover design by Saxton Randolph
Interior design and typesetting by HR Hegnauer
Text set in Perpetua and Helsinki

Cataloging-in-publication data is available from the Library of Congress

Nightboat Books
New York
www.nightboat.org

# YOU AND I

[NO COLONIAL]

[POST COLONIAL]

you and I have never left ~~Nigeria~~ ~~Biafra~~
Yorubaland. I raise a house of children in between
kissing the maid on her lips. you,
kissing me, too. I write poems in lotion
pools in the small of your back after
our children fall asleep under the mosquito
nets. a tree drops soft fragrant fruit onto
our roof. we hear ripe thuds
in the night's quiet. I am still afraid of
snakes. bodies without limbs unsettle
me until my final days. we witness
as revolution crumbles America,
it wilts in our own city, the world
expands, and collapses
beneath our Black hands, my life
behind a memory of a colonial reality
you don't remember. each morning you wake,
your lips, your chest, your hands come down
on top of me and I flinch, remembering,
before I indulge your gentleness.

the cramped apartment space we share in
these rooms, three stories up. I threaten,
secretly take a capsule every day to keep
my children waiting in either side room.
forcing penetration tires you. it only seems
droning to me, and my eyelashes cast
your lips in shadow. you admit to being
only one inch above me in height,
your physical failure. it's how you comfort
my supposed barrenness. you eat
all your body will allow, and I persist.
I throw out all the gifts my body
could birth you. the day my attraction
wanes. I begin to love you, and my world
shrinks. it's the size of a human
taller than myself and all the people who
walk from my womb. I am all but
a plunging flourish of starlings
saturating the sky above in disquiet
through a partition made of circumstance.

# I NEVER USED TO WRITE ABOUT BIRDS

falling out of the sky
I must have had freedom
      and lost it in my rush
to pick through the ambrosia

bone and crust the divine
throw down to us when the sun
      betrays their secret
luminous banquet

        when gold dust collects
            in their feather threads
        against the cusp of dusk

        the birds fall from flight
            design forsaken and punctuate
        the surface of Lake Michigan

waves rush filling
the broken compromise
      between flight and matter
every nerve I own

is swelling to golden hour's
      haze and plummet litany

        it's time to glow
        up in praise of the stars
            burning gainless
        and the sun tracing clouds

        in renaissance oil paint
            praise where the sky cracks
        open to its interior the backlit ozone

this is the closest I'll get to grabbing
          our unjust god by the pearls
strung across his throat so I can ask

why he sat back in luster
          all these millennia
watching my people die

## SPLAY MY COUNTRY ☆

<pre>
                         this is how I feel
        small and significant                    when you blow me over
                      like topsoil dusting a bulb
           small enough to live          inside my mother
                   a piece of genetic scrap metal
        a prayer another planet's sun dust         goods where the umbra
    and nettle thicket amass                    I have forsaken my view
              of the cosmos for sprawls      of aureole-donning steel
                      I meant nothing and I still do
             but now the nothing         comes disguised
                      as neon drowning orion
        in blush every night                    and another day leaning back
                    to die against the skyline
             built to hold every gaze      bound for the heavens
                   the city's refusal to migrate
        into me and me begging                    its black harmony
                      to keep chanting
              I'm sighing open          spiral compounds
            for what men build          what we risk in unison
</pre>

4

# NEVER HAVE I EVER

*dated a Black person* - my father 2019


never knowing
        the sun's blue genus

lipped along the back
as the light of a new day

        presses infinitesimal color
into the both of you

there is for me no other
way to tether love

between this vessel
        and the lucent spools

I cast against an ocean's skin
at the hull of me latent lyrics

        at the helm an onyx compass
-wielding child

villageless in all their wanting

# GIRL CRUSH

I'm the first god born by mother's assertion

*she wants to be just like her*

                              *like her*

            *like her*

like the girls in track pants and navel rings

in fond pursuit I loved myself

if she's me I can always hold her

# POEM WHERE I REFUSE TO TALK ABOUT ███████

I'm eight wearing a frumpy
bunched-up dress with stockings
I put runs in that same morning
while rushing to pull them up
after peeing and flattening
my midweek temple frizz
the cool girls in their jeans
and angel|devil T's are having
a laugh at my existence
they are white and built like
miniature bird-chested women
on asphalt my low heels
clacking like principal feet
I want the sweat of boyhood
its ease and virtue on my neck
I want my nature known
because I am the softest
I can ever be in this moment
when I don't rough my mutt
hands on their throats
for making terrible light of
the second-hand the sub
-human my survival
instead I talk to grass
but a sapling myself
I am made everyday like a bed
like a person makes another
and nothing ever asks to be made

*free verse*
*narrative ballad / lyric*
*distinctive style*
*confessional*
*enjambment protest*
*Agency*
*exposed through*
*"I"*
*words*
*related to*
*agency*

# CLASSIFICATION AND DISSECTION ⭐

The mulatto walks on two legs,

        has two arms, a thorax, three

gills on either side of the trachea,

        and two hands to run

the blood mill frothing in its chest.

While the mulatto is substantiated

on the cornmeal vows of white parents,

and the pent-up won't-says of Black ones,

the mulatto is comprised mostly of

effervescent elements not yet documented.

Superstitious and vengeful, the mulatto has been

        known to sever a farmstead from its clement winds.


Remember, the mulatto eye is speculative and hung

        up on the horn of nostalgia, the gut-shot rites knighting


Black men in robes of flame when rumored

        they take up with white women.

The phoenix should not come

                    to mind. The mulatto is the fire's wake

dressed in ash, not a winged contender

                    cheating death match after match.

# SOCIAL DEATH, AN ADDRESS

I write to you from the predicament of Blackness.

You see, I've been here all my life and found,

on the atomic level, it's impossible to walk through

most doorways. I can, however, move through

walls. I write to you from the empty seat that isn't

empty. I write to you when a feel is copped.

I write myself out of bed. I write to you as the spook

who sat by the door. I write to you from Olivia

Pope's apolitical mouth. I am here because I could

never get the hang of body death, though it has been

presented to me like one would offer a roofied cocktail

or high-interest loan. I am only here because I started

eating again. I am only here because I am ineligible

to exist otherwise. I'm only here because I left and

returned through an Atlantic wormhole. I write to you as

the American version of me. In the American version,

Orpheus' lyre is a gun. Eurydice thinks of doctors,

or, rather a cold hand. It feels like one is sliding its sterile nails over the curtains of her womb. Once, a healer's hands

passed through my flesh, and I went on trial for stealing

ten fingers. When my spoon scrapes the bottom of a bowl

it sounds like a choir of siblings naming stars after their favorite

meals. Physicists are classifying new matters and energies

every day. Dark matter, Black flesh are in high demand,

and we never see a penny. I urge you. If you see a sister

walk through walls or survive the un-survivable, sip your

drink and learn to forget or love the taxed apparition before you.

# THEY WANT BLACK MUSIC AND THEY DON'T WANT BLACK PEOPLE

                                        like to parse mirth from flesh


play us to drown out the meek

sounds of their love-making

this is how they worship            pent until welling

                                     my wife's song

                                     on their wife's tongue


the mouth is a most hated negro

attribute and somehow it births

a coveted forte so searing          their eyes hang

                                     a heavy velvet ribbon

                                     over the keyhole

# CAPTIVITY LESSONS ☆

In the dream where we switch places I barricade
myself in the wine cellar while you run through
my home in a dress made of flames. You make
quick work of the brittle wood, snapping support
beams. In this realm, the estate alights with the massacre
of inverse, we both know privacy and rape.

My skin is night-water black where
your shadow falls over me. The commute
to bondage was sickening. You see these dead
limbs? You see these pearls? Everything I need
is in another hemisphere. Everyone I love is here.

I take care not to swallow the children
I carry in my mouth. Some of them mine,
some of them yours. None of them
will learn my tongue. They are all so close
to dying the same way, it makes my mouth water.

You pull meat off the bone, raw.
The flesh surrounds you in rot. Flies walk
across your eyes as if they are iced-over lakes.
Your home is infested. Is this a metaphor
for Europe? you'll ask when you read this.
I blink for you. I close my eyes on your behalf.

# ODE TO A VIBRATOR LEFT ON ALL NIGHT

In her absence, my hunger for hum
and throttle took me by sweltering longitude.

For the right to claim shotgun I drove
a stick through the streets of Osu

while a man steered, yielding to clutch,
pressing us further into night.

I know well the sound, engine's
purring plea for shift, and my hand the abundance

of submission. I withheld nothing. I want when
I want, and then I wish for corrosion.

Though I cannot lavish praise on stamina
alone, I must acknowledge a femme

fortitude. Last night, I tell myself,
a misstep at battery's expense

so as to never consider the sentience
of a pleasure machine.

How her trembling must have lullabied
my drunk tongue the intricacies

of sexual decorum even in sleep,
how she may have throbbed

all night beside me, anticipating her
own reciprocal and tender invasion.

16

# INTIMATE ARCHIVES

If you were to hang yourself, you wouldn't die, you don't know how to die.

DAWN LUNDY MARTIN

## THE GOOD SHIP JESUS

you and I spoke the same language so we cursed
and sang and closed each other's mouths to
preserve our water. with the ocean at our backs
we shuffled through piles of death

and then you were in that pile, but I never
stopped talking to you, not even after I found
my legs, not even after I found my pupils
refused to shrink in their want for gathering darkness.

## ELMINA CASTLE

at first only the rivers and I wept
for you in your journey, like the waters'
from tropical interiors, to the estuary
slap of the ocean's cupped hands

and then your absence became religion
as easily as creating meaning from loss of limb,
you fell into crates that rustled from within
to the tune of the wind's phantom chorale

## WAR ON DRUGS

somebody drove into our part of town and left
a truck full of shivers. lilac vibrations at first,
and to cease touching them to our mouths,
as was our habit, throttled us into convulsions.

you, me and even our infant shook
like diamonds around the neck of a runaway
queen. somebody took us apart, not limb by
limb, or shake from shudder, but kin from akin

# MONTICELLO

outside our bed, everything was kissing
or biting you in the name of disgust, in
the name of labor, in the name of flesh
breaking, and babies being born

the man never did smile in his portraits,
but by the pitch of your cries, by the perse
abrasions on your throat, Sally, I knew
he had a set of teeth.

## DR. J. MARION SIMS' HOSPITAL FOR WOMEN

when your callused hand warmed itself
between my thighs from behind, I recoiled
from our mating ritual. you were hurt, sour
as a boy suppered without meat.

I wanted to tell you that I was hewn today
by an assortment of cutlery. there was only
me and the doctor and there was only whiskey
to keep my cries from outing themselves.

## ANGOLA PENITENTIARY

I am the one who visits you, and I swallow
a key for every year you're put away.
I swallow our entire home, stuff
books and television shows into my pockets.

before I can slip you a single comfort
between your teeth they pick me up, shake
me, and confiscate everything on my person
into a box labeled CONTRABAND.

## TULSA "THE BLACK WALL STREET" BOMBING ☆

we consummated our marriage
on a bed littered with the sour faces
of dead presidents, liberated livestock
sweating through the dollars.

call it loot looting its owner, or the lack
of snow on our lawns last winter,
the blue sky overhead now pitching
an ammo lethal as white discontent.

## THE TUSKEGEE EXPERIMENTS

in a fit, you slapped my fingers to your
forehead and asked me to pull off the horns
growing from it. despite their absence,
I told you these horns were lovely.

someone told you that eating chicken would
shrink your brain and dry out your skin,
but there wasn't much else lying around,
so I called it duck to grease open your lips.

## NORPLANT

the doctors put rods in your arm to confuse
your hormones. the deal: you give up your
hospitable womb, and they remove
the bars from your window.

but the rods made you bleed for months
at a time. when leaving the house was no
longer an option, I cut six holes in your skin
and drew out each branch with my mouth.

# BLACK BODY AS TOLD BY THE STIRRUPS

Thank you for your cooperation  The soft bow of your heel
The air pushed open by your leg span  Do you remember
when we met  How no drugs were administered
How the hands that opened you were cold
and soiled  How the unsurgical steel slid
you open easy as an envelope  How
you dilated between my grasp  Feel
the wind warp through you
keyhole to chimney
You cow into
disrobe

You off
your layers  Slump
down the table resenting
proximity  The hands are still
ice and white melting into your folds
Your trickle-down DNA blotting the hissing
sheet  The flinch in your breast  You would have
swallowed the hand mirror to avoid me  You want
to turn yourself over  Press the hard cotton gown into
your gums  You turn yourself over to spread and capture
to ensure the tameless animal stays put between your thighs

# ANARCHA AND I NEGOTIATE TRAUMA

Anarcha passed me hers by her teeth and I nearly choked making space for her mammoth seed alongside mine. I trusted her with a mouth too full to speak. I trusted her to slide something flora inside of me. The first time I felt another person's desire it was pressed on my leg and this leg was pinned to the couch. In so wanting to tell this, I pitted my mouth twice. There was meat initially on the peaches that we halved off and fed to each other making sure to miss the mouth enough for the lips and neighboring skin to get sweet and wet. Anarcha had impassioned arguments with me, that brought me to trembling. I never wanted to nutcracker someone's head with my thighs so badly. She told me the children knocked the latch off her bladder when they sprang from her. She told me her body was living, when it was hewn for science, but she wanted to be taken with and by me. Around the pits, I said, I am a poet and a queer and I cannot real-estate a bit more of my tongue to doctors or men. And with this heavy mouth, I spouted these words in whale song. Inaudible. Why don't you spit those out, she said, so I can hear the yes that's under all that need?

# HULL ☆

I gulp into
my lungs for
a few cents of
oxygen. It is for the
dead's inability to do so
that I rattle the coins in my
chest. In every exhale there
is audacity. Some of us still drown
in our own lungs. We are in need of a
plan. Let's deflate something monstrous,
and take its air inside us. I'm holding quorum
between my sternum and the equator for survival
lessons. Here I learn my skin on hers won't liberate us,

and I begin
to touch her
as though it will,
remembering fat to be
an unruly flesh, our uprising
lungs a cacophony of inverted
sound. Only when there was nothing
left to sing did the hull-song quiet to breath.
By the flush of a roseate moon, a ship presses
its belly into the Atlantic's lap. At this tempo, persons
breach objectivity, and must then revert back. The objects
approach personhood. I won't count breaths as the cargo cusps
in continuum, a salient stain on the horizon that never makes port.

so        hungered    were    we    for    we    known

and       favored    spice    for    we    yam

and    goat    and    coiled    red    pepper    to

bless    we    gullets    we    sank    teeth

below    skin    in    we    assembled    flesh    how

we    bit    air    to    breathe    how    we

fed    on    sharks    that    so    readily

feasted    on    we    flesh    we    took

night    in    we    mouths    when    we    counted

the    one    swelling    celestial    basin    the

grains    of    rice    gluttoned    over    the    evening's

belly    more    than    one    of    we

collapsed    from    the    weight    bloated    on    hours

mistaken    for    a    single    endless    nightfall

we    shook    we    we    mixed    we    tongues

rollicked    vowels    over    every    body    and

so    hungered    were    we    for    ritual    in

we    lives    we    paid    homage    to

we    menses    by    fingering    this    blood

across    we    backs    as    it    arrived

as    we    lived    bleeding    by    the    day

count    of    we    organs    motioned    hands

towards    we    waxing    clock    we    proved    nothing

we    fixed    we    selves    to    we

by        the        choice        of        clutch        we        put

    we        whole        minds        in        we        fingertips

and        lived        in        the        heat        frictioned        bodies

    house        so        hungered        were        we        for

expanse        and        spread        and        quiet        that        not

    I        but        some        of        we        we

viced        breath        from        we        gasped        to        stillness

    until        I        been        told        there        was

a        weightless        feeling        either        way        but        those

    of        we        in        line        with        slaying

became        suns        pulling        cold        heavenly        bodies        into

    distressed        rotation

# MICHELLE OBAMA AND I SELF-MEDICATE

Anxiety has clawed a red highway up my esophagus, and for this Michelle suggests chamomile. She knows where these red routes can lead. My palms feel hotter than the inside of my mouth. There are no handles or surfaces to relieve us. I want to drop this comfort, but Michelle is telling me about how He doesn't close his eyes anymore when they make love, how no one closes their eyes around her anymore, so I ask her if she'd like me to close my eyes. My hands are rocking the cup between blistering fingers and she says, yes, so I do. I feel or I imagine The First Lady's fingers everywhere, or perhaps it is her breath. The generations of flowers beheaded for blooming out of season, and my latent disordered eating are a few of the things flaming my gullet. Michelle tells me she can't remember the last time she touched someone who didn't need to make sure she was there. Do you want to leave? I ask. I want you to drink your tea, she tells me, feeling the way my body hums like a coffee bean. I lift the chamomile to my mouth and taste without seeing. My tongue becomes a burning house. I know what I am feeling is her chest rising and falling against my back. She smells how I expect a ripe cotton field must.

# I LIKE THE COLD

L
but only for

R
the sweetness

M
provided the body

R
upon its return

L
to warmth

R
I spend so much

M
time alone

R
I don't know

L
how to ration

R
the hot stars

M
in my fingertips

L
for you they all come

R
splendor-forth

M
and dripping in tar

*free verse*
*monostitch*
*enjambment*
*lyrical*
*1 to 4 beat*
*rhythm*

have you ever heard

of intimate space

compounding with want

it suckled our first tryst

candied in a history

long before      it called out to you

I learned to make

my own heat

23

# DAD JACKET ☆

if Chicago is still

    breaking me in

        with its weather

and tethered eye

    you be the arch

        in my neck

the mane

    growing from it

        and the wind

running through it

    with you I be

        rampant as a joke

off a tongue

    that's off the clock

        when my master

come as the cold

    wet the leering

        staggering men

I ask I be insulate

    and I ask I be

        invisible like a tuber

or a sock

    gagging on its kin

        in a swell of beige

and you

    sweat-spent and

        tattered sleet smart

serving second term

    fold me in

        a new way

# WANT COULD KILL ME

I know this

from looking

        into store fronts

        taste buds voguing

alight from the way

treasure glows

        when I imagine

        pressing its opulence

into your hand

I want to buy you

        a cobalt velvet couch

        all your haters' teeth

strung up like pearls

a cannabis vineyard

        and plane tickets

        to every island

on earth

but my pockets

        are filled with

        lint and love alone

touch these inanimate gods

to my eyelids

        when you kiss me

        linen leather

gator skin silk

satin lace onyx

        marble gold ferns

        leopard crystal

sandalwood mink

pearl stiletto

        matte nails and plush

        lips glossed

in my 90s baby saliva

pour the glitter

        over my bare skin

        I want a lavish life

us in the crook

of a hammock

        incensed by romance

        the bowerbird will

forgo rest and meals

so he may primp

        and anticipate amenity

        for his singing lover

call me a gaunt bird

a keeper of altars

                    shrines to the tactile


                    how they shine for you
fold your wings

around my shoulders

                    promise me that


                    should I drown
in want-made waste

the dress I sink in

                    will be exquisite


*for Dominique*

## OPULENCE

my heaven innard

turned to land

    apostled lips

gilding sonnets

    I wanted to

claim her

    I was wrong

to wander inward

    translucent centipede

trusting head bone
    with thistle feet

I too danced

    through her

eardrum and sank

    to her feet

stilled to basking

    when love leaves

the flesh and becomes

    the broth of light

# EDMONIA LEWIS AND I WEATHER THE STORM

The places where Edmonia's bones were fractured still hold violent reverberations. When it rains I massage the static hum out of each point of impact. There is nothing heavier than flesh that wishes to be on another axis, except perhaps stone she shaped. Tonight she tells me, it's impossible to bring a lover to the small death she deserves. An orgasm is excavated, never given. She takes my face in her hands without permission. I take her waist with care not to treat her like a healing thing. She is digging me out of my misery with her fugitive hands. No one has ever led me out of myself the way she does. She makes a pocket of me until I cry. I've seen that field, the site of her breaking, in the empty parking lot I cut through to class. There is nothing left for us to forge in Oberlin, and still we remain, Edmonia a sentient rock, swallowing her own feet in want of motion. We fit on this twin sized bed only by entanglement. We survive here by the brine of our brutish blood.

# TWO-HEADED SLAKE

You take the tongue I speak       and make me beg it back
                                  into my head. Without language,
        I'm a man stranded and walking
                                  barefoot. No nuance. A goat
bleating its way home       in the dark. I labor sound,
                                  a braying siren sans time
        signature. You ask of me
                                  mid-theft, and I
translate beasted litany:       They're building a podium
                                  to disclose my animalia
        from. Wooing valleys
                                  where my names lived,
waxed, and fermented       their sigil into the sunken
                                  earth. In me they built you
        a home with a porch swing
                                  out back. You colonist,
carry me over my threshold.       Run up the stairs and run
                                  back down. Be thorough.
        Before the windows distill
                                  to fog-licked pelt, turn on
every single light in this       good damned house.

# SEX DREAM IN THE KEY OF APORIA

I half-wake in sudor, queer vernacular forgotten in the sinew of sleep.
Wetted by a man whose saunter turns
         my breed diaphanous,

I fasten myself to his shared anatomies while he ascribes me
to the shades of children we'd make.
         Sex, my choice

harness for affection, I falter before unreining curiosity.
Trans time and space,
         I follow the russet roads inside myself,

Accra lanced into my neural system still. My intra-continent sweats
through shirts, and drinks stout,
         though it tastes of displacement.

I still have a penchant for what misconstrued me, to live among kin in exclusion.
Awake, I don't conflate touch with knowledge,
         so my projected selves approach

the helm as nimbus parts me. Their mission is simple.
I buck their tether.
         They tighten its hold.

# ERICA GARNER AND JOHN HENRY(ISM) SAID ☆

this hammer

and oyster knife

this weaponized praxis

and bound whet acumen

build backfiring crossbow

I'm spent and every arrow

that doesn't claim me

names me

I'll die with a hammer

in my hand

asthma in my aria

and impulse thrumming

my labor nerve numb

bootstraps fondled

in impatience

are themselves

tiny nooses

how many cells

in my body

committed suicide today

tell me this

and I'll build

an underground

fire escape

                              every molecule

serves an abortive god

laying tendon in blood route

when I stake my shoulders

against the steel sinew

                              of the state

worth becomes

a deadly trait

to demonstrate

# SARA BAARTMAN AND I FOLD LAUNDRY

I hate to fold in public, but Sara insists that the clothes must be tended to when they are fresh from the dryer. Side-by-side at this laundromat, our hips brush while we arrange our clothes. We fold our panties differently. Hers in two, like closing a silk book; mine in a tri-fold. A man behind us snickers and I turn. His phallus is exposed through the open mouth of his zipper: a premature eggplant still umbilicaled, condensed in color, more night sky than mature purple. He looks at both of us and back down at his produce. I hate to fold in public. Sara turns too and laughs. She walks up to him. For a moment I wince thinking of his flesh caught in the metal teeth of his jeans, but she reaches down the front of her own shirt. He looks at me while she chases something she's hidden between her breasts. A single dollar bill falls out and onto the grey tiled floor. For the show, she says, before returning to me and teasing a hug out from under my crossed arms.

# FOR A BURIAL FREE OF SHARKS

how        in        the        hull        we        worked        we

   wormed        at        earth's        lack        in        we

lives        and        in        those        deaths        and        I

   say        we        not        collective        not        tongued

the        same        and        not        kin        and        not

   in        love        but        in        all        of

we        pressed        up        against        we        heat        and

   doings        similar        and        reduced        to        sameness

saw        the        first        of        we        plunging

   for        home        landing        in        a        shiver

of        them        saw        the        moon        waxing        pink

   with        carnage        we        may        have        known

well        I        did        not        that        a        drop

   would        not        take        we        to        the

bottom        and        buried        we        had        to        try

   to        die        better        without        soil        to

pollinate        pores        no        soul        restoration        some        of

   we        we        risked        death        to        put

dead        in        the        ground        we        worked        we

   wormed        we        did        we        pieces        for

a        burial        free        of        sharks        the        earth

   was        sand        a        sea        kind        of

solid        a        half        after-life        we        thought        was

   better        but        tides        did        rise        and sharks    uncovered    what    we    hands    put    over

    we    found    we    bodies    to    devour

failure    to    send    we    home    was    not

    without    punishment    one    of    we    not

I    was    tethered    ankles    to    hull    and

    we    saw    this    one    we    disappear

by    limb    until    there    was    only    a

    pair    of    feet    trailing    the    ship

I    still    haven't    a    want    for    death

    though    my    burial    impends    we    all

been    too    physical    flesh    is    the    closest

    ground    in    sight    putting    the    mind

on    a    high    shelf    is    a    burial

    without    sharks    I    double    where    my

joints    can    and    bury    self    in    self

# NATURE POEM WITH COMPULSIVE ATTRACTION TO THE SHARK

the hive swells outside
as its residents itch to lick our inner walls

for moisture and respite

from January's cold appendages
                    nature    having thrummed
on its own
blood and grace for millenia

until ours—a short tailored tenure
a blip in comparison to the shark

more ancient than trees
killing only to feed

moving so it will not die
it wants only what the sea has brined

the shark does not know
                        implication

violence fades to nimbus
depletes blue to red the tides

where pleas parch the lips of tempest
the terror in the land the terror at sea

on the eve of our industrial revolution
made weapon of hungry thing

I've heard this slave
song before

boats from across the ocean escorting
these mature predators in swarms

mouths that hungered about

        the taste of slaves

men and sharks parting at shore
shaking with a taste for each other

turning the word with every tide
the currents lap at my latent limb

every volta America wrote
        for me had teeth

        won't you allow me now
to lift my lip and show you mine

## THE MASTER'S TOOLS

I hold this temporary sweetness in my mouth
a small wedge lopped off the mother melon
still tethered to the grove

watermelon is a social fruit
with many heads to a single spine

       watermelon is a social fruit
I press its meat to your waterbed mouth

in your eyes I see the tool shed on fire
we won't need the spades the anvil
heavy as a blue whale's heart

you kiss me and the fruit look
like swollen bodies in a chain gang

       you kiss me so deep I might never leave
the fields I've been leashed to

we bear no laborers
to wither with this empire

our instruments of desire chafe a blue flame
the thicket swelling with us to ash

we're not here to dismantle anything
we've come to burn the big house down

# VESTER FLANAGAN AND I ESCAPE VIRGINIA

When I ask about his life in Roanoke, Vester tells me, I avoided mixing

in society, and wrapped myself in mystery, devoting my time to fasting and prayer. His Turnerian

language has me thinking about slave revolts. Vester did a white thing

when he didn't flay his own body first. The enslaved live

so differently now, can it truly compare? Overly attentive to metaphor, I conclude yes, as he

foots the gas pedal in his Chevrolet Sonic pushing the two of us past

the speed limit on 1-77 North. We drove down Plantation Road one last time. My God. I thought it would all end there a few times. My hands are red with Flamin' Hot dust and I feel errant as a runaway. Only one of us wanted, both of us gunning for change. I nearly lost my truth in Blacksburg. He asks me to imagine a future awaiting our starved mouths before it is bitten into, before hands can lay filth to it, to sleep in the cut corners of rings, rims of bottles, and stained glass steamed by the breath of song. Lyric and madness spooning in the driver's seat. Another soft brown thing in this world resisting. On this sticky matter I can only sing: captive folk of ritual. folk of grinding teeth. folk of homespun poison. I have a right to my anger at a landscape and the people who inhabit it. It's in the air tendering the skin, wading the hairs on the back of my neck. Peripheral lords rasping like moths against a rusted screen. In every era, in every state, no violence is the same. Somehow all of it feels intimate. Vester did a slave thing. A color line in the distance calls out to us. We humor our asymptote syndrome. It says, I'm the horizon and I'm waiting.

# STRESS DREAM IN THE KEY OF PROZAC ✷

I know the dead walk
depressive body roll
Sethe dancing when Beloved
tried to ghost her to death
the heartbeat buried in
the thigh meat—patent it
flick a Baldwinian wrist
send a tempest to my country
as the Lorde demands it by
uses of the erotic the erotic
as power outages stemming
from electric areola and
street light shattering moan
this war waits for no one
but when it does it hides
in the panty drawer
the war comes out of me
when the night is pregnant I'm walking on a beach
with someone else's
social prowess
the war comes out of me
makes the mattress
cutting board
beneath my carnal jaw
cosign the beasts to being
for the feeding on master
descended flesh
blue-boned inheritance
parse the wolves from men
cradling soul salt locker
the ocean is rife with slave

rebellious dead if you
believe in empire
when the ocean is turnt
on haint jabbering
sharks who swam
and fed until they too
lived in diaspora
may those teeth lost lead to
splendor and marrow
devour us before
we eat all the trees
I do not eat the men
without skin
I want her face
a hot thing
I'm speaking
in Morrison
with two men
one I pretend to love
one I pretend not to
my muggy inlet
basin of semen
basin of red clay earth
I say to them both
the sycamores beat out
the children every time
I make them watch me
unfasten myself from
my yolk of repression
gild the ocean in doubt

# NATIVITY

in the dream where I run without breasts I am motivated by flight, I haven't yet begun to un-
weld the framework, invent new trauma, whip the stitch arching each bosom as victuals dan-
gled, withheld. when I hemorrhage against design it ain't incognito. the neighbors walk their
dogs past me. that's me smoking in the alley, letting roses from my wrists. petal to puddle,
a misgendering of matter. these hooves unhinge themselves as tiny meteors to cudgel dusk. I
redress the splintering woodwork notched to my likeness, venial beneath the pomme and lilac
cornucopic delight. to partake in a gender, to fashion one's self a living process of it, casting a
net of postures, adornment objects, and grooming techniques into a future tense. where have
I gone, and who have I built to take my place? unsuccessful at the tossing of it, I throw rocks
ahead of me and predict where they will land. by virtue of touch, I am every man I manufacture
my difference from. the man slipping in the mirror's moonshine enters and leaves me between
my double-take. every night the countryside plays against my eyelids. a recurring taunt against
my current location, the finale, currents of corn lapping the sun against my arms pumping with
youth. the site of my making.

# SOMETIMES BOYHOOD

hovering their mouths

        like two men

        moments before

    they turn on each other

that is how the grass smells

        need between boys

        I wanted a love like

    a shared look

so relieved to be touching

        so angry it took so long

        too easy to rehearse into fragility

    as a boy I couldn't hide

a single soft thing

        round with lemon skin

        under her shirt

    silken folds of fat

the boy thinks

        she is a canal for shame

where goodness ends

the scent of new blood

a red scout of longing

through her private dimension

the boy tables girlhood

and the sweat is good sweat

a flock of braying gestures

shaving september grains

a cunning hunt

for each other's touch

two men sparring

over who could end

the other's suffering first

bliss shame from the body

was I not one of them

disarming a denim ilk

praying his sword would land

amidst my vast acreage

# NO ONE SPEAKS OF HOW TENDRILS FEED ON THE FRUITS

no one speaks of how tendrils feed on the fruits

of my demise     these dead hands                    for instance   that alight phlox

wild strawberry                    and pine       this is my body out of context   rotting in the wrong

hemisphere   I died    so all my enemies would tremble at my murmur       how it populates

their homes   so I could say to the nearest fellow dead person   *I know more than all my living*

*foes*       I've derived sun-sustained design                    for once       from closing

my oak eyes           now they'll never snare the civilian

pullulating my throat

# A FRUIT WE NEVER TASTED ☆

we          carried          the          ocean          across          fault          we

named we eyes after anything          that could conjure a body          of water from its head

we          carried          the          ocean          a          ledger

traced in salt          we rife with          homeland drupe pineapple mango ripening to split

its          own          parrot          skin          and          weeping          tongues

hacked to former          we become  rotten teeth plucked          from howling jaws

when          we          carried          the          ocean          to

we sod and slatted lean-tos          we death huts          sold into shacks

we          blistered          we          split-back          houses          we          hot

blank speech          we passed ocean between we          by the throat

we          defoliate          we          worked          we          wormed

on the land on the bodies of fruit we never tasted          when we set to swell          and soften the

rice          it          takes          gallons          more          water          to

boil the ocean we owe for swallowing yesterday water          we did not  retch

but          I          have          felt          a          churn

since          taking the shoes of a man hanged          how his feet pendulumed a     dancing     shadow's     final     hue     decays     resolve

blueing the land in eulogy          we work until we work eventual we the grind

summoning     a     fruit     we     never     tasted

# NOTES

"Social Death, An Address" stylistically nods to Terrance Hayes' "Lighthead's Guide to the Galaxy."

In "Vester Flanagan and I Escape Virginia," Nat Turner is quoted directly: "I avoided mixing in society, and wrapped myself in mystery, devoting my time to fasting and prayer."

"Stress Dream in the Key of Prozac" quotes short passages from Toni Morrison's *Beloved*.

# ACKNOWLEDGMENTS

Many thanks to the folks who run Nightboat Books for your trust and support.

Thank you to the editors of these literary journals and anthologies where poems in *HULL* first appeared, sometimes with different names or forms:

*The Account*, *American Poetry Review*, *ANMLY*, *Black Warrior Review*, *Beloit Poetry Journal*, *The BreakBeat Poets Vol. 2: Black Girl Magic*, *Crazyhorse*, *Day One*, *GIGANTIC Sequins*, *The James Franco Review*, *LAMBDA Literary*, *Nashville Review*, *Nat. Brut*, *Nepantla: An Anthology of Queer Poets of Color*, *Ninth Letter*, *The Offing*, *Poets.org*, *Qu Literary Journal*, *Scalawag*, *The Shade Journal*, *The Shallow Ends*, *Virginia Quarterly Review*, and *Yalobusha Review*.

Poems from this collection have also appeared in the chapbook *Reasons for Smoking* (Seattle Review, 2017).

To my teachers: Dawn, Erika, Evie, Kazim, Vievee, and Willie, I thank you for your illumination and guidance.

I have infinite gratitude for Chekwube Danladi, Tafisha Edwards, Marwa Helal, Taylor Johnson, Sarah Maria Medina, Cheswayo Mphanza, and Justin Phillip Reed, my friends who have also been my editors.

Thank you Alison, Amber, Andriniki, Annabel, Breauna, Camonghne, Casey, Charleen, Cortney, Devyn, Eloisa, francine, Hanif, Inam, Jan, Jari, Jayson, jazz, Jonah, Joseph, Joshua, LG, Lisa, Luther, mai, Monica, Nabila, Nicholas, Paula, Raven, Raych, Saida, Samiya, Sylvie, and Yasmin for helping me feel seen through this process. Our encounters have been blessings.

Without the love and support of my mother, father, and sister, Olivia, this book would not exist. I must extend a thank you, as well, to my chosen family members: Brannon, Chekwube, Dominique, Jen, Kris, Johanna, Marwa, Milo, Tiesha, and Valerie—any tenderness achieved in this book is a testament to the love my families and communities have shown me.

XANDRIA PHILLIPS is a poet and visual artist from rural Ohio. They are the author of *Reasons for Smoking*, and the poetry editor of *Winter Tangerine*. Xandria has received fellowships from Cave Canem, Callaloo, and the Wisconsin Institute for Creative Writing, where they are the First Wave Poetry Fellow. Their poetry has been featured in *Black Warrior Review*, *Crazyhorse*, *Poets.org*, *Virginia Quarterly Review*, and elsewhere.

# NIGHTBOAT BOOKS

Nightboat Books, a nonprofit organization, seeks to develop audiences for writers whose work resists convention and transcends boundaries. We publish books rich with poignancy, intelligence, and risk. Please visit nightboat.org to learn about our titles and how you can support our future publications.

The following individuals have supported the publication of this book. We thank them for their generosity and commitment to the mission of Nightboat Books:

Kazim Ali
Anonymous
Jean C. Ballantyne
Photios Giovanis
Amanda Greenberger
Elizabeth Motika
Benjamin Taylor
Peter Waldor
Jerrie Whitfield & Richard Motika

Nightboat Books gratefully acknowledges support from the National Endowment for the Arts.

# HULL